ADAPT AND OVERCOME

An Entrepreneur's Tactical Guide to Winning in Business

STEVE SCHABACKER

Adapt and Overcome: An Entrepreneur's Tactical Guide to Winning in Business

ISBN: 978-0-578-35274-9

Cover design by Sooraj Mats

Edited by Hilary Jastram & Dave Rynne, www.jhilcreative.com

DEDICATION

To my best friend and partner in crime, Katrina. I would not be where I am today without you. I will love you forever and a day.

Resources

To access massive resources and tactical coaching programs from Steve and his team, please visit:

www.TacticalEntrepreneurAcademy.com

Follow Steve and get in touch

Personal Facebook Page
Facebook.com/Steve.Schabacker

The Tactical Entrepreneur Podcast Facebook Page
Facebook.com/TacticalEntrepreneur

Sheepdog Firearms Facebook Page
Facebook.com/SheepDogAcademy

Instagram
Instagram.com/Steve_Schabacker_Official

The Tactical Entrepreneur Podcast Page
Instagram.com/TacticalEntrepreneur

Sheepdog Firearms Page
Instagram.com/SheepDogFirearms

Press Kit
SteveSchabacker.com/PressKit

Table of Contents

FOREWORD

If you were to ask ten random people on the street if they've ever thought about writing a book, all ten of them would unanimously answer yes. But if you immediately asked them right after that, "Have you written a book?" all ten of them would say no.

It's very rare to meet a published author, especially in this day and age. It's very rare to meet another human being who has had the patience to sit down behind a typewriter, computer, or even a smartphone—and design, articulate, put together, and publish an entire book.

Let me tell you; it's no easy feat. Still, it's something that almost everyone of sound mind dreams of doing at some point in their life. But almost no one actually does it.

That's the difference between a guy like Steve Schabacker and other folks: He doesn't just talk about what he's going to do; he takes action on it.

I'll never forget the first time I met Steve; he had come to one of our Apex mastermind meetings and introduced himself to me. He shook my hand, looked me right in the face, and said that he was going to be an example for this network.

I hear that all the time, and oftentimes, the person who says it means it—but there's a difference between the person who says something and actually means it. And there's a difference between that person and the person who says something, means it *and* does it.

I continued to watch Steve come in over the next year and a half, and every time he was a little bit leaner, a little bit more confident, a little bit better in business, and a little bit better in life. Most importantly, he was happier. Over the course of 14 months, I watched a man transform from what was seemingly impossible to a man living a life that was not only possible, but he was actually experiencing it every day.

This man had transformed right before my eyes. Seeing these changes in him reminded me of our first conversation when he said he was going to represent. I'm telling you, as a friend, a mentor—a person who cares about Steve—this is a guy who represents what winning looks like at all times.

This is a guy who represents the results of hard work at all times. A guy who wasn't handed anything but had to claw his way up to get everything he's ever wanted.

My kind of guy.

You're about to read that story in this book. You're about to learn firsthand the experiences, lessons and wisdom of a man who has outworked almost everybody I have come into contact with.

It's very fortunate that you're here.

Fortunate because you either bought this book or someone who cares about you and wants to see you succeed gave it to you.

Fortunate because if you don't already know Steve through social media, you're going to get to know him through this book.

Fortunate because you can take these life lessons and convert them into your own—and take action on them.

Rise above,
Ryan Stewman

Introduction

"Good is good enough."

"There is nothing wrong with the status quo."

"If it ain't broke, don't fix it."

"It has always been done this way."

The statements above are all lies. They are lies that we tell ourselves and other people to justify many of our actions. Well, our lack of action mostly. Entrepreneurs are often the biggest offenders in the use of those statements. The reasons for this can be anything from laziness, not wanting to ruffle feathers, or simply not thinking out of the box.

In the competitive marketplace that exists today, the company that differentiates itself will often lead the way in both sales and growth. This is true in almost any industry that exists. If you plan on doing things the same way as the competition, why even bother? You won't be helping your potential customers or yourself.

What if I told you there was a better way?

A method that would allow you to be different, new, and fresh no matter how old the industry is. A method that would help your business grow, get more customers, and create more revenue. Would you be interested? This book will give you the information needed to do exactly that. It will teach you to *Adapt and Overcome* by finding the gaps in your industry and using them to your advantage.

Now, I know what you are thinking:

- It can't work in my industry.

- It will be too hard.

- Everyone in my industry does things the same way.

Those are nothing more than excuses. The process is actually very simple, but it is not easy. It will require work on your part, and for you to be brutally honest with yourself. If you can commit to those two things and follow the instructions given the results will come. If you can't, please do me a favor and give this book to someone who cares about their customers and wants to leave a legacy.

You are still here! Great!

I'm glad we are on the same page. Before we get to work, I want to give you a little background on this pro-

Ready to get work?

Sit down, strap in, and hang on. This is going to be quite the ride.

CHAPTER ONE

THE SECRET SAUCE

"Play by the rules, but be ferocious."
—Phil Knight

There's only one fact you need to know that will change everything about your life and business ... It's an insider hack that once you learn it, you will never not use it to get and stay ahead.

Scratch that.

This book is no fairy tale.

I am going to tell you how it really is to be an entrepreneur. The ups and downs. The truth.

All of it.

If you are thinking of starting your own business or you have been in business for yourself for a little while, you need to know the truth so you can get and feel prepared.

I wish I had been prepared. That someone had laid it all out on the line for me. That's the experience I hope you have in reading this book.

This book will give you an actionable plan on how to protect and grow your business during good times, tough times—even a pandemic, and anywhere in between.

The title of this chapter, "Secret Sauce," was meant to deceive you. It was chosen to get you reading the book. You probably thought, *WOW, this guy is going to throw it all out there in chapter one"*. While I am not going to spill the secret sauce just yet, I am going to lay the background for our journey together ahead.

MY "NORMAL" JOB

Ever since I can remember, I have not been content working a normal job.

I've had a few jobs over the years, from working as a telephone operator for a long distance carrier to building furniture to even inspecting supercomputer chips. I'm a fast learner and excel at most any job. But I become bored quickly, so I would always look for a new department to transfer to or additional responsibilities to take on. It didn't matter what job I wound up taking or where I moved in a company; I never found fulfillment. That clued me in that there was something different about me, but I had no idea what.

From a young age, I'd been taught that the "goal" in life was to find a good company, stay there for 35 or 40 years, and then retire. In the beginning of my working career, I bought in to this plan, although I was curious about many of the small businesses I saw starting up. Still, I never gave launching a company of my own any serious thought. The idea was squashed pretty quickly anyway since I'd been assured by my family while growing up that there is "no security in that" and "it was just too risky."

Fast forward to 2008, I had been with a custom audio video installation company in Chicago for about four years. I started out as an installation team leader, then worked my way up to service tech, then custom sales engineer and finally project manager. To climb this ladder, I attended advanced training in acoustics, system design, control system programming, and video calibration.

I led teams doing installs in the homes of celebrities, professional athletes, and business moguls all around Chicagoland. This was a great job for me at the time. I was making a good living, had fairly regular hours, and enjoyed it very much. I did not think life could get much better.

Then one day, out of the blue, I was called into the conference room by the company owners and my direct manager—the COO. I did not see the crushing blow coming. They explained that business was down and my position was being eliminated.

It came like a swift kick in the nuts. *Wait, what?* I thought as my mind scrambled to make sense of what they'd told me. So many emotions hit me all at once. To this day, I'm not sure how I fought off the urge to tell them to go fuck themselves hard.

Getting let go was tough.
What I had to do next was 1000% tougher.

On a busy Friday afternoon, I was wrapping up the week and trying to play catch up. I had put in some long hours between the many projects going on at work and my eldest daughter Kayleigh being in and out of the hospital. I was ready to finish it up and hopefully have time to stop and breathe a bit. Suddenly my boss Tom walked into the office I shared with a couple of other employees.

He said, "Steve, we need to see you in the conference room right away." I had no idea what was about to happen, but as I entered the conference room with a pit in my stomach, I noticed Tom was not alone. Both owners of the company were also present.

I instantly realized this was no normal meeting. While I was not sure exactly what was about to go down, I knew it likely was not good. The tension was high in the room.

I sat down in an uncomfortable chair across from the three of them. The lights seemed so bright, they almost hurt my eyes.

Tom started in right away: "This was not an easy decision, Steve. but we are going to be making some changes."

My heart hammered in my chest as he continued to explain that business was slowing down and the company no longer needed my project management services.

These were some of the most overwhelming words I had ever heard.

It was all also happening at the worst time possible in my life. At that moment, I cried as I had not done in years —right there in the conference room.

When I went home, I had to break it to my wife Katrina that I did not have a job and we would be losing our health insurance. Losing health insurance is bad, but in our case, it was terrible.

At the time, our eldest daughter Kayleigh had been in and out of the hospital for a strange condition that the doctors couldn't diagnose. I'll get back to her story in a later chapter. For now, all you need to know is that I was panicked. *I just can't let everyone down*, was all I could think.

For several months after that big talk at the conference table, I felt sorry for myself. Then I got busy and applied for jobs that landed me exactly zero calls for interviews. I felt as worthless as a man could, angry at myself and God. My frustration, depression, and fury got worse with each passing day.

Soon, I was in such a dark place I wasn't sure I could get out.

What saved me was deep diving into the analysis of the situation. I relived it in my head over and over again and picked apart every last detail to make sure I would never put myself in that situation ever again. In the end, I concluded that the only one I could trust to not lay me off again was me. That terrible meeting kicked off the long journey of becoming who I am today.

LIFE RESET

I had no idea what I wanted to do, how I was going to do it, or where to start. In my circle of friends and family, I had nowhere to go for support, no one to ask questions, and no road map to follow. All I knew was that I wanted to start a business for myself. One way or another, I had to figure it out.

Choosing this path brought out some of the coldest comments from friends, family and even acquaintances. Comments like "So you aren't going to get another job?" and "How do you expect to provide for your family without one?" and even "Man, you need to grow up. You have kids to take care of."

What I expected was absolutely the opposite of what I received. I expected people to be happy for me and supportive, but I received very little of that. The only one I could count on was my wife Katrina. While she did not understand my desire to pave my own path, she had my back.

But I have since learned that how I was treated is quite common among others on this journey.

If you decide to become an entrepreneur, you will likely feel very alone and question yourself often. As I shared, your family might ask when you are going to get a "real job." There will be constant roadblocks, trials, and tribulations. You will lose a lot of sleep and experience many setbacks. There is a real possibility that it will also impact relationships with your friends, family, and possibly your spouse.

But if you stick with running your business, you will feel fulfilled in knowing that you are in control of your destiny. If you are willing to commit to constantly learning, staying focused, and a ton of hard work, you can create the future you desire.

The process I am going to teach you in this book is one I have used myself, and taught others to use many times. It works in any industry and on businesses of all sizes. It makes the hardships of entrepreneurship easier, which is why I rely on it and teach it to other people. My objective is to provide support and let you know that this road can be less rocky when you know the tricks of the trade.

Once you master this system and the tools contained in it, you will likely sleep better at night, too, knowing that you can conquer anything thrown your way.

Throughout the rest of this book, we will focus on your path ahead. No matter what stage you are at in your business, you will learn the tools that will give you a tactical advantage over your personal challenges and the challenges that spring up outside of your business.

It will not be easy. It will require hard work, a large investment in time, and being brutally honest with yourself—but you can achieve anything you desire if you are willing to go all-in on yourself and your future.

Facta non Verba (Actions speak louder than words). If you have ever seen my social media posts, heard me speak, or watched any of my online trainings you will recognize this statement. It is more than words. It is the battle cry I live by.

Talking about doing this or doing that is the easy part. Taking action is what most struggle with. You see, people are full crap much more often than they will admit.

But if you want to stand out in the crowd—simply do the work, don't make excuses, and you will. It's simple but it is not easy.

Now, that's enough talk. It's time to take action!

TACTICAL TAKEAWAYS

- Your life can change in the blink of an eye. You must be ready for anything.

- The old saying "That which does not kill you makes you stronger" is absolutely true. Overcoming challenges sharpens your mind and body.

- Don't talk about doing something. DO IT!

CHAPTER TWO

ASSESS THE SITUATION

"I'm here to build something for the long-term. Anything else is a distraction."
—*Mark Zuckerberg*

Before you can get where you want to go in your business, you need to do a brutal, honest assessment of it.

What are the facts you need to know?

Where are you right now?

Where do you want to go?

You can answer these questions by learning the three key parts of your business that you must get crystal clear about.

The Importance of Being Honest

Before we get started, there is one key expectation I have of you.

I expect that you will stop lying.

I'm not saying that you lie to others all the time, but you likely lie to yourself.

Lying to yourself can involve everything from having an overly optimistic outlook to rounding the numbers up a bit or even being in downright denial about what you could be doing better. For your business to work, you must be 100% honest with yourself. Can you commit to that? If not, stop reading and give this book away to someone who could use the methods I am sharing with you.

No words written here will do you any benefit if your actions are not based on truth.

Do You Know Who You Serve?

Before you do anything else in your business, you need to know your customer. I mean, REALLY know them. A statement such as "My customers are middle-aged men" is way too vague.

First: Drill down into who your customers are as if you're trying to describe their qualities funneled into a single person. Do this in such detail that it describes the core of their being. This exercise is commonly referred to as building your customer avatar.

Your customer avatar will constantly evolve and get more detailed as you go through the process of defining it. There are many ways to work through this exercise and get great results. I like to start with the basics and then get more specific as I go.

Please understand the importance of this exercise.

If you do not take the time to get your customer avatar right, it will make many things more difficult or impossible in your business. The customer avatar is the key foundation that you will build your marketing and sales processes around. Your business will depend on it. I created a template to help you with this exercise that will provide clarity and make the process much easier.

You can find my interactive guide to building your customer here: www.TacticalEntrepreneurAcademy.com/Resources

Through answering a series of questions and entering the key traits your ideal customers exhibit, you will create a working model of who your perfect customer is. Once you become completely clear on that, you can then figure out exactly where to find many more of them. It's best to put down this book, complete the exercise, then come back to the book once your avatar has been created.

*****

Welcome back.

Even if doing that exercise was a little bit harder than you expected, I want to assure you that your effort will be well worth it.

What you just created will be the key to understanding your customers better.

This information will also be priceless when planning your marketing campaigns. That's because the better you know your customer, the easier it will be for you to find more of them. Ideally, you even need to know your customers better than you know yourself.

Second: Know your one, five, and ten-year targets.

When you read that, you might have thought: *I have no idea where I want to be in ten years.*

That is unacceptable.

Make it a priority to figure out where you stand and do it quick. These directions are a two-sided process. You need to know where you are right now, but you also need to decide where you want to end up. Once you have your current location and your target location defined, it's a much easier process.

Did you notice I did not say goal? I used the word "target" for a reason.

That's because goals are bullshit. The word itself gives you an out. It creates the expectation that your aim doesn't need to be reached every time.

We hit goals *sometimes*, like in soccer. Targets are hit *every time*. Sure, the hit may not be perfect, but it is still a hit. In Navy SEAL Teams they say, "Aim Small. Miss Small." What they mean is that you need a very specific target to aim for. The more specific your target, the more likely you are to hit it or get very close.

There are many ways to create your targets. I used to struggle with this until I figured out the easy way. Yes, thankfully there's a shortcut to eliminating needless pain.

The first step is to figure out your pipe dream, otherwise known as the ten-year target. This dream *must* seem totally unattainable. Take some time and think about where you believe you can be in your business in ten years. Do you see it?

Now double or triple it.

You can do it even if your first inclination is to think you can't.

This dream should seem so totally far-fetched that you think you have no chance in hell of hitting it. It should be so out of the stratosphere that you get bonus points for each time you get called crazy to your face when sharing it with others.

After you have identified your dream, don't worry about how you are going to do it. Simply worry about *what* it is you want to accomplish.

When completing this exercise there are a few things to remember. First, there is no wrong answer. Your target is your target. It is yours alone. What is important to you surrounding this target may not matter to others—and that is okay. Don't let that stop you from having your big dream.

Be assured it's okay to dream HUGE. Give yourself permission to leave everything on the table and ALL your options open.

Don't forget, imperfect action beats perfect thought every single time. Your ten-year plan will often be very agile as changes happen frequently around you. This is to be expected and embraced.

With your ten-year target clearly defined, let's figure out what your five-year milestone should be. Perhaps your target falls right in the middle of your timeline, but most of the time, it is less than halfway. In the beginning, movement will be slower until you pick up momentum. Once you get into a rhythm or flow, your progress will happen much faster. You will likely accomplish the final 75% of your progress in the same amount of time as the first 25%.

Once your five-year target is in place, it's time to figure out your one-year target. This one will likely seem much more attainable than the others, but figuring out this one will actually be the toughest.

When you start out, and you're trying to put parameters around this target, you will not have the momentum to help you. So, you must claw, scratch, and drag yourself along to get started.

This process and way of assessing your business will seem very strange. I assure you, if you stick to the plan you have laid out for yourself, it will get easier and clearer each day. Your process won't stop at the one-year level, either, but will get more detailed. I will explain more about this concept later in the book.

Third: Know your key performance indicators (KPIs). These KPIs could be a group of the most common measurements, but they should be customized to your business, industry, and overall targets. KPIs ensure you are viewing a clear picture of your current situation in regard to a specific area of your business.

Let's assume we are looking at two different businesses. One business operates a brick-and-mortar retail store, while the other is run strictly online. Looking at sales per square foot would be very useful for the brick-and-mortar store but useless to the online store. On the other hand, a KPI such as a conversion rate is critical to the online store but equally meaningless to the brick-and-mortar store.

I suggest identifying or creating around four to six KPIs that will serve your business best. These will be your starting points but could change as you refine your business or change your focus. Here are a few of the common KPIs I use in some of my businesses.

KPIs

CASH FLOW FORECAST

This KPI is arguably the most important piece of data for many small businesses. Identifying problems in this area is critical to keeping your business on the right track. Running out of cash is not something that can be remedied on the fly and must be planned for well in advance. Cash flow is the cause of many small business failures.

SALES FUNNEL DROP OFF

This KPI is usually a critical metric, but the areas it examines vary for different types of business. For example, an online B2C business will use it to assess stats around "abandoned cart" or "abandoned browse." In a B2B business, the sales funnel may be managed by a sales manager. The KPI in this instance will measure milestones such as needs identified, proposals given, and closes. Understanding the metrics of completed sales versus how many people start the process can provide a clearer understanding of the effectiveness of your sales funnel. Figuring out where people are making the decision to not complete their purchase, why they are not completing it, and what you can do to bring them back can make a huge difference to your bottom line. It will also help to expose weaknesses in price structure, value proposition, and many other areas.

INVENTORY TURNOVER

This KPI is mandatory for any business selling physical goods. You need to know it for several reasons. Different industries have different lead times for their products, but they all typically need inventory available to sell. While you want to have product available, you also don't want to have too much in stock as that can have a negative impact on available cash and credit.

RELATIVE MARKET SHARE

This is pretty self-explanatory but don't let the simplicity of the title fool you. This KPI measures how much of a given market you control. The other assessments we talked about are based on internal factors, while relative market share is an external metric that evaluates how you are doing compared to your competitors. Using this metric over time can help you deploy changes in your products, pricing, or marketing strategies to grow your market share. This metric will constantly change as moves are made by you and your competitors. It can be a complex process to analyze the change and determine what made the change happen, but the effort can change the outcome of your business.

There are literally dozens of other common KPIs in business that you may want to explore and even more that are custom to some industries. The common ones are talked about often and can be calculated by accounting software. The more specialized KPIs may need to be calculated or an Excel spreadsheet that has been specially formulated can do it for you.

SWOT Analysis

Once I have dug into the KPIs, I like to use a SWOT analysis to gain perspective inside and outside the business. I document what I find in a standardized manner using a form I've created. You can download a copy of the form here and use it to help you:

www.tacticalentrepreneuracademy.com/swotform

SWOT stands for

- Strengths

- Weaknesses

- Opportunities

- Threats

Consider these key points when executing each portion of the analysis. These categories could potentially have many different types of answers.

To ensure I am covering all my bases, I take each one of the following topics and examine my first initial thoughts before doing a deeper dive into them.

- Finance

- Operations

- Market Conditions

- Sales and Marketing

Next, I will view each of these subjects through the lens of the leader in the organization who would be in charge of them. For example, if I was looking through the finance lens, I would put myself in the position of the CFO to discover what they might uncover. I would do the same for every SWOT area, writing down anything of interest or anything unusual that I would need to look into further. If I find a weakness that could be construed as more intense than I might anticipate, I would then work to understand why that is. You want to know every part of your business implicitly.

STRENGTHS

Analyzing your strengths may sound very simple on the surface but going deeper is where the magic happens. Strengths in finance might mean a strong cash flow, good margins, or perhaps a great new line of credit. Strengths in operations could mean having solid systems in place or improving efficiency. Market condition strengths might involve increased demand or competitors closing their doors. Sales and marketing could include simply getting leads or closing sales.

WEAKNESSES

Dissecting your weaknesses can be painful, but it is necessary. It is also possible to be strong in some areas and weak in others. For example, you may have noted "good margins" in your strengths and "poor cash flow" in your weaknesses as it pertains to finance. Rarely is a topic *all* strong or *all* weak. Common weaknesses in operations could include employee churn, vendor issues, or customer service problems.

OPPORTUNITIES

In the category of Opportunities things get interesting. While strengths and weaknesses are important, they don't directly provide fruit. Identified opportunities can be directly used for growth. This part of the SWOT analysis requires looking inside and outside your organization at the same time. On the inside, there may be internal opportunities for improvements in efficiency or even expansion. On the outside, there may be gaps in the marketplace, chances to move into new geographical areas, or even to grow through the acquisition of competitors. In this section, it is especially important to think outside the box, and not take anything off the table—even if it seems silly or irrelevant at the time. Some opportunities are easy to see, but others require some digging. When assessing opportunities, remember that any opportunity exists in that moment of time. Opportunities can look great on a particular day, but may not be possible even the next day. Speed wins over perfection every time. Seize and leverage timely opportunities so you don't lose them.

THREATS

Threats are similar to opportunities in that they also require looking both inside and outside your organization. One common example of an internal threat would be the loss of key employees. Outside your company, you might experience threats from your competition. A new or existing competitor in town could take market share from you, for instance.

It is critical to be aware of threats but equally important to not waste your time ruminating. The knowledge of threats can help when formulating future plans, but in the end, it is important to focus more on your own company than what others are doing. In many situations, we are our own worst enemies and can stop forward momentum before we even get started.

SWOT analysis is a powerful tool that you can use to discover deep truths about your business, internally and externally. Like many other tools in life, it is only as good as the effort that you put into it. Taking your time and being thorough are the keys to using it successfully.

TACTICAL TAKEAWAYS

- Be brutally honest with yourself. Without the truth nothing in this chapter will work.

- Know your customer and everything about them. Be crystal clear on who you serve and why.

- Know your KPIs. They will provide a clear picture of exactly where you are at any point in time. These are the facts regarding the health of your business. Ignore your feelings and focus on the facts.

- Be clear on your one-year, five-year and ten-year plans. Without a plan the direction of your business has no chance of succeeding.

Are you starting to see how powerful it is to always be analyzing and assessing?

We discuss these and many other lessons on The Tactical Entrepreneur Podcast at TacticalEntrepreneurPodcast.com.

CHAPTER THREE

FIND THE GAP

"You've got to look for a gap,
where competitors in a market have grown lazy
and lost contact with the readers or viewers."
—*Rupert Murdoch*

Have you ever heard the phrase "It's better to be lucky than good"? I'm not sure I would prefer luck over talent but in the case of what I am about to tell you, everything worked out great.

In early 2018, I owned companies in several different industries including private security and investigations as well as IT managed services and cyber security. My team and I were quite busy and business was going well on all fronts. The last thing we probably needed was another company to worry about.

We were several years into a successful security and investigations company. In the state of Illinois, any security guard or private investigator needing to carry a firearm while on the job must go through a 40-hour training. This presented a logical opportunity for us.

With most of our clients wanting us to provide armed guards for their facilities, we decided to train our guards in-house how to do that so we could be sure they were trained to our standards. One of my partners in the security company was also a chief of police and had taught firearms for years. He was the perfect person to be our primary instructor. We purchased a portable training range housed in a semi-trailer and got to work.

Around this time, concealed carry licensing had finally been created in the state of Illinois. This license required a 16-hour training class with a mix of classroom and range training. Many friends and business associates asked if we were going to offer this training as they knew we had the range and that we trained our security guards.

In the beginning, we said no as we thought training would be a distraction to the main mission of our business. Then people asked us about it so often that we decided to do a class or two just to shut everyone up. After the first couple of classes, we gained so much momentum that we kept doing them. The classes then took on a life of their own as the demand went through the roof and we could hardly keep up.

Through these classes, we had the opportunity to have conversations with many people. They loved our training but kept asking us to expand our service offerings into other areas of the firearms industry. They also expressed their unhappiness with the current state of gun shops in the area. The more we talked to people, the more we heard about what they wanted more of.

In the Chicagoland area, there were two general types of shops, and most people did not really like either of these models.

On one side of the spectrum, was the large chain shops that were basically like a Walmart for guns. They were large, mostly clean, and had decent prices, but the customer service and general knowledge were not there.

On the other side of the spectrum were the small shops with wood paneling, various dead animals on the walls, and two grumpy old guys behind the counter. When you walked in, you rarely felt welcome. If you did not look the way they expected, talk the way they expected, or were not an older male—you would feel uncomfortable fast. You also had about five minutes to decide what you wanted, or get out. There was absolutely zero customer focus and even less customer service.

We believed that a firearms store could be created where people of all ages, experience levels, sexes, races—and even political parties—could come. Everyone would be welcomed regardless of their firearm knowledge and experience. From this vision, the idea for Sheepdog Firearms was born.

In Sun Tzu's book *The Art of War*, he says, "Be where your enemy is not." That is a great example of what I mean by finding the gap.

When going into or trying to succeed in any business, you must have a differentiator.

The "enemy" Tzu refers to is your competition. If you do not fill this gap with your services, you will likely fail. Sheepdog's differentiator was clear. We knew exactly what we wanted to do and just needed to fill in the details of how we were going to do it.

You may be thinking, *but Steve, that strategy won't work in my industry*. To that, I say "bullshit." It absolutely will work. It's just a matter of finding the gap to exploit. To help you with that process, you can use the following steps to help you formulate a plan.

YOUR PLAN TO DIFFERENTIATE YOUR BUSINESS

STEP ONE: ASSESS YOUR COMPETITION

Just as we took a hard look at where you are in your business using a number of tools in the previous chapter, now we must look at the competition. When doing this, push yourself to think big.

Don't worry about the competitors that you already dominate; focus on the bigger fish, the ones you get uncomfortable comparing yourself to. Pick at least three or four of your best competitors for this exercise and purchase their products or services.

If they are online, place an order; if they are a brick-and-mortar store, shop there.

Once you've done that, its's time to get brutally honest with yourself and answer the questions below:

1. How was the buying experience? (What was good and what was not?)

2. How does the product compare to your offerings: Price, quality, style, and so on?

3. How was their communication with you as a customer?

4. What do they do better than you do?

5. What do you do better than they do?

After you have completed the assessment of your competitors, head to step two.

STEP TWO: ANALYZE

With the assessments of the competition and your SWOT analysis completed, it is time to look at the data. To see the results clearly, I prefer to organize the data into a spreadsheet so I can compare all the competitors in side-by-side scenarios. A simple version using the example of a local restaurant may look like this:

	COMPETITOR			
	A	**B**	**C**	**D**
Style	sit down - casual	sit down - formal	take out only	fast casual
Food Quality	good	excellent	poor	satisfactory
Menu Variety	excellent	satisfactory	poor	satisfactory
Menu Specifics	burgers, wings, salads	steaks, pasta	pizza, grinders	burgers, fries
Value	good	good	satisfactory	excellent

	COMPETITOR			
	A	**B**	**C**	**D**
Service	poor - order mistakes	poor - very slow	satisfactory	poor
Speed / Convenience	poor	poor	satisfactory	poor
Entertainment	live music	none	none	none
Theme	none	romantic	none	50's diner
Alcohol	no - byob allowed	no	no	no
Dine In Seating	yes	yes	no	yes - no waitstaff
Carryout Available	yes	no	yes	yes
Delivery Available	no	no	no	no

In this table, you can see each of the competitors is different. They all have their strengths and weaknesses, but when you directly contrast these companies, a gap may become clear.

In this example, a couple of gaps stick out.

One example could be what style of food is served. Have you noticed that no local place has seafood on its menu? Perhaps you've realized that while there are a couple of places with similar menus as the restaurant being compared, none of them serve alcohol. Or maybe the service level is more evident to you, and you see an opportunity such as doing takeout—especially if none of the competitors are offering it. I would consider any of these differences as meeting in-the-box, or common, criteria.

Trying to focus on the less common differences can be a bit harder but also more rewarding. You have to be willing to suspend reality for a moment and let anything be possible. To delve deeper into this scenario, I will stay with the restaurant theme but pick an interesting spot from Chicago.

If you have not heard of Ed Debevic's *Diner* and stumbled upon it by accident, you would be very surprised. The place is always packed, even though the food is mediocre at best.

Why, you ask?

It's the entertainment that comes along with your meal … whether you ask for it or not.

Ed Debevic's is known for their rude waitresses and the side of harassment that comes with your meal. People come from all over the place for the combo comedy bit and cheeseburger. This out-of-the-box blend created a place that diners *seek* out. It's not something I would have ever thought of, but it turned out great for Ed's.

Step Three: Choose Your Hole:

After analyzing where the holes are, you need to decide how you will fill the hole that best suits you. You must commit when you say you will fill that hole. While it is important to be thorough in your analyzing the situation, paralysis by analysis is a real issue to be conscious of. Hesitation, delay, or second-guessing yourself will lead to failure. So, decide, then take action. Make no excuses about getting to work!

When choosing your path, a delicate balance of risk versus reward is in play. Often, the more you risk by straying from the perceived norms in your industry, the bigger the possible gain.

In the case of Sheepdog, in addition to the differences I spoke about earlier, we also decided to design the layout in a completely unique way.

As the CMO (chief marketing officer), I pushed hard during the design process to make Sheepdog a signature experience. I aimed to include as much of the Sheepdog story into the overall design as possible. This included trying some layout options that hadn't been done before. At least, I had never heard about them.

I wanted the Sheepdog theme to be part of the store and give the whole space a story. The place had to be more interesting and welcoming than paneling on the walls with dead animals staring down at you with their glassy eyes.

The design concept would start with a controlled area where customers were shown firearms. The typical gun shop has rows of glass cases with firearms inside. If you want to handle a firearm, you have to know exactly what it is you want to see in order to have it pulled out from behind the glass. This means customers with no specific shopping list can have an extremely hard time.

After showing you two or three guns, the clerk will often lose patience and expect you to make a choice. But what if you are a new gun owner and have zero idea what you want or what gun would fit you best? Normally, the clerk would give you what he thinks you should try.

Sometimes you end up with the best firearm for you, but often, you don't.

In my vision for Sheepdog, I thought there could be a better way to create the ability to handle many firearms and see what fits in your hand the best. There would also be no pressure on the clerk to keep taking out firearms, making shopping a lower-pressure and more pleasant experience. Enter the Sheepdog Kennel.

In keeping with our theme, the gun area was made to resemble a large dog kennel. A chain-link fence ran all the way up to the ceiling; the concrete floor was finished in a raw concrete look and a gate was put in place for security. Customers could walk in, handle all the firearms they wanted, ask any questions, and make a choice at their pace.

Fast forward to now, and The Kennel has become one of the key differentiators of Sheepdog.

It is this novel design that has led to many repeat customers. While it is completely different and out of the ordinary, it has also helped Sheepdog go from zero sales to $2M per year in revenue in just over two years. Understand, we are a 900-square-foot store located in a secluded area with almost zero drive-by traffic, so we know this innovative concept is working for us.

When choosing your gap, it is critical to leave all options on the table. Don't throw out any idea. Sometimes the best gap you find might seem silly at first. In our restaurant scenario above, some common differentiators could be service, food quality, and atmosphere. Less common but possibly equally important factors could be theme, entertainment, speed of service, location, and price.

You can often choose multiple correct directions. There is not necessarily one right choice that would make all the rest wrong. Timing can be a big part of the equation. You and your team need to be ready for the change and actually realize you need it.

Situations and landscapes can change quickly in any industry, too; therefore accurate and timely information is key. Because of the potential of dynamics to change, I recommend you do the assessments immediately before you choose the path.

Now, it's time to find your gap and get ready to fill it. This is the fun part as your new direction can fall into place quickly.

TACTICAL TAKEAWAYS

- You must differentiate your business.
- There are many ways to be different. Pick one that resonates with you.
- Let your vision and mission lead you.
- There can be multiple correct answers to the same question.

CHAPTER FOUR

DESIGN THE MISSION

*"There are dreamers, and there are planners;
the planners make their dreams come true."*
—*Edwin Louis Cole*

Now that your current situation is crystal clear and your gap is identified, it is time to focus and capitalize on it.

Having a clear plan makes all the difference in business and life. When you have a plan all mapped out, it is much easier to feel comfortable where you are, even if you don't yet have all the details required for your plan.

Which brings me to a time I had no answers and was scared out of my mind.

Every Parent's Nightmare

As a father, it is one thing when things you cannot control happen to you, but it is quite another when what you can't control happens to one of your children.

That is absolutely the worst feeling ever.

It was a typical summer evening. My eldest daughter Kayleigh was thirteen at the time and in the middle of her softball season. She was playing an away game in a nearby town that was a short drive from our house.

The game was nothing out of the ordinary, and it was a beautiful night out … until we hit the midway point. That's when Kayleigh suddenly collapsed. Running as fast as I could, yet seemingly in slow motion I raced over to her as another parent called 911. My wife Katrina was in shock. Kayleigh was completely unconscious but was breathing and had a pulse. The paramedics arrived after what seemed like an eternity but, in reality, was only a couple of minutes.

They began working on her and transported her by ambulance to the nearest hospital. Katrina rode with her, and I followed the ambulance in our car.

Everything was still moving in slow motion, and I had so many thoughts running through my head. *Was she okay? Why wasn't the ambulance driving faster? How could this even be happening?*

When we got to the emergency room, Kayleigh was coming back around, but she was very dazed and confused. She did not remember any of it. I was relieved to see her conscious but did not believe she was out of the woods yet. The doctors ran what seemed like neverending tests that all indicated nothing was wrong. All her doctors were stumped as to what had happened but were convinced that Kayleigh was fine.

She was released from the hospital with no answers but we were overjoyed to take her home regardless.

Over the next couple of weeks, Kayleigh had many more of these episodes and was transported each time by ambulance to the hospital. Sometimes, she had them while at home and another time she had one when we were out running errands.

Each time the doctors had no idea what was going on. They just and kept saying she was fine, although they believed she was having seizures of some sort. Every time it happened we became more and more concerned.

During many of the episodes, Kayleigh's eyes stayed open, but she was clearly not there. As the episodes continued, she became very aware of when they were about to happen (often several times a day). They started with a feeling that her throat was closing, and it was hard to breathe. She had no power over them but at least could feel them enough in advance to lie down and avoid a fall. After many trips to different doctors and hospitals, Katrina and I knew Kayleigh needed extreme treatment. We had to get to the bottom of why she was ill. Her condition simply could not be allowed to continue with no end in sight.

We could not allow our little girl to live like this.

The doctors that treated her believed it was neurological, so we started to research hospitals and chose Comer Children's Hospital in Chicago because it had great specialists in the field Kayleigh needed. Choosing the hospital was the easy part. Actually getting Kayleigh there was much harder. After sharing our frustrations with her family physician, he helped us by reaching out to Comer and getting them to accept her case. We were hoping this was truly the light at the end of the tunnel.

Arriving at Comer was a whirlwind experience in the best way possible. Kayleigh bypassed the ER and was taken right to the neurological floor for admission. Upon her arrival, she was greeted by one of the residents on call and made to feel at home —as much as possible in a hospital anyway. The resident asked a ton of questions and documented all Kayleigh's symptoms and the way they came on. Katrina and I began to feel a little more at ease. It seemed like she was in the right place.

Fast forward to the next morning, when we met her care team. This was a seemingly endless stream of doctors and all their groups of residents. There were so many it was hard to tell who was in charge until one of the awesome nurses clued us in. This was when we learned a trick about how you could tell who was who. She told us, "The longer the lab coat, the higher up the chain of command." Sure enough, we found that the person with the longest lab coat was almost always the one speaking to us.

After meeting with the different teams representing Neurology, Infectious Disease, General Practice, and more departments that I can't remember, a couple of the head doctors came back to talk to us.

While they didn't know what was wrong, they did articulate a thorough plan to rule out specific conditions. They would run a series of tests over the next few days that they said should ultimately find the issue. A feeling of calm came over Katrina and me. We did not have a solution, but we finally had a plan.

That night, I slept on probably the most uncomfortable couch the hospital owned but had the best rest I'd experienced in weeks. The weight of the unknown had been partially lifted.

Don't think there was a happy ending just yet. It was not that easy. I promise, I will finish Kayleigh's story in a later chapter. For now, I want you to focus on the main lesson: Life can look up through merely having a plan.

HAVE A PLAN TO GROW YOUR BUSINESS

In Chapter Three, we talked about assessing your operation and the competition to see how you stack up against each other. Through this assessment, you found your gap to exploit. Now that we know your gap let's make a plan to use it to your advantage.

Before you start planning, allow me to make one thing clear: We are not seeking perfection. We are seeking massive action.

Good is good enough, and as Sheryl Sandberg, the COO of Facebook states, "Done is better than perfect."

Be clear laying out your plan, but be sure to avoid analysis paralysis. Meaning, it's easy to get caught in mental masturbation and not get a damn thing done. The best action to take if you find yourself stuck is to get your plan on paper. To better explain what I mean, let's use the restaurant in the table in Chapter Two to start to build our sample plan.

YOUR FIRST STEP

Start with the gap you found, then use it to your advantage. In the case of our restaurant, the gap I identified was the service aspect of the dining experience. When looking through the table, this revealed itself to me as a huge opportunity. While the restaurant was not a fine dining establishment by any means, there was still an opportunity to make their differentiation stronger through new service offerings.

We knew there were several possible gaps, but the service option appeared to have the greatest opportunity. When looking at the table comparison, we can see that the food quality and variety are equal. But the theme of the restaurant and what they provided for was lacking compared to other nearby options. Convenience and speed could have been possibilities to improve upon, but I passed them over because they could be easily replicated by the competition.

After the mission in your plan is clear, it's time to flush out the specifics.

We know we want to crush the competition through outstanding service and to do that, we need to know exactly what that looks like including what needs to happen and who is in charge.

During this process, it is vital to get the input and view of what you are trying to do from key staff members. This will help get the buy-in you will need from them later on during the implementation, and it's crucial that these pivotal people believe in what you are doing as much as you do. Remember, they can provide you with additional perspectives. For example, the executive chef may view specific areas of interest differently than the front of house manager.

Having input from these players not only maintains buy-in, but it also gives you great input from those handling operations in certain areas.

Here is an example of specifics that could be included to help achieve the overall mission making the restaurant more successful by providing a superior dining experience.

PERSONALIZATION
••

Using the Open Table platform, we will start a campaign to encourage our customers to make reservations. This can be accomplished in a number of ways. In addition, using a combination of methods would likely provide the greatest results. These methods can include targeted Facebook ads, emails to existing customers, offering incentives and coupons through third-party dining apps, and traditional print marketing.

Through this campaign, we can learn more about our customers, how often they return and what they like. We will enable Open Table to allow customers to communicate a preferred table type or area of seating when they come eat at the restaurant. Our hostess will consistently welcome the customers and convey that we are happy they are here. The hostess will also communicate any relevant information such as names, celebrations, and any other details that can be used to make the client feel at home.

TEAMWORK
••

Servers and support staff will be monetarily incentivized to work as a team and think of every table as theirs versus the usual model of assigning one specific server to a table. Compensation will also be shifted by the sharing of tips which will further incentivize the team atmosphere and everyone taking ownership of all diners. The staff will learn quickly that the more their diners have a great experience, the more the tip pool will grow. This enables the staff to win together. This mentality will create a different environment than is commonly witnessed in most restaurants. It will also likely require changes in personnel as shift managers may identify resistant individuals. We will move forward and provide opportunities for individuals to choose their path—whether that be to stay and continue working at the restaurant or to leave and find another job elsewhere.

CHOREOGRAPHY

Each part of the dining experience will be a perfectly choreographed dance. Servers and support staff will move together in time. The kitchen will have its timing down to a science. The dining experience will become consistent regardless of day, time, server, or any other variable. This will enable the timing of reservations to stay on schedule and patrons to know exactly what to expect. The best service does not stick out but instead blends in.

Traditionally, in most restaurants very little thought is given to consistency of timing. Some industries are exceptional at it by design. A cruise ship is a great example of this. Due to the amount of people they serve daily, a higher level of scheduling must be used. We can learn a lot from this practice and apply it to a traditional establishment on land.

Normally much of the choreography we can observe in a more traditional restaurant varies by server. This makes it much more difficult to maintain consistency. For example, one server may put in entrees at the same time as an appetizer while other servers may delay putting in the main course—if they want to get their appetizer on a diner's table.

ANTICIPATION

Servers and staff will work to anticipate patrons' needs and fulfill those needs without being asked. Refills will magically appear. A dropped utensil will be replaced before the diner can ask. The removal of emptied plates will be smooth and efficient. By staying one step ahead, we can provide outstanding service.

Using these four main pillars, the restaurant will become a place people can return to predicated on the way it makes them *feel*. They will likely have consumed better food somewhere else, or had a better atmosphere at times, but they will *never* have better service.

The target is making each person feel like they are the most important person in the restaurant to us. Every. Single. Time.

This plan provides an effective framework that is the foundation of the process, allowing us to continue to instill initiatives.

With that piece of the puzzle snapped into place, it's time to move on to who is going to be responsible for each role and be the go-to person who will ensure each step is completed according to the plan. This is not a plan to be implemented in one day, and it's not based on using it in a specific time frame. Your new plan requires the development of the processes you need and continuous implementation.

With the overall mission plan in play, we can move on to the next step: Creating the rules of engagement (ROE), which I will cover in the next chapter.

TACTICAL TAKEAWAYS

- Have a plan.

- Good is good enough and done is better than perfect.

- Think of the customer experience first.

Do you like what you are reading?

Check out a ton of similar lessons on The Tactical Entrepreneur Podcast at www.TacticalEntrepreneurPodcast.com

CHAPTER FIVE

RULES OF ENGAGEMENT

"Risk comes from not knowing
what you are doing."
—Warren Buffett

Remember Kayleigh's story that I started to tell you in the last chapter? Here's how the ending played out.

WHAT WAS WRONG?

With Kayleigh at Comer Children's Hospital, Katrina and I switched off staying with her at all times. We told her she would not be alone and come hell or high water, we made sure of that. We juggled our jobs, our two other children at home, and an unbelievable amount of stress. Still, we set one foot in front of the other and moved forward the best we could.

Days went by, test after test was taken, yet there was no clear progress or even a cause as to what was going on with her. The doctors were getting nowhere. Then they decided to go back to the basics and recheck what had been done.

They realized she had not been tested for Lyme disease so they administered that blood test.

The next thing we knew it came back positive. There was a cause. Infectious disease doctors came in and spoke with us about the results. The good news was that they'd found something, but the test alone could not determine if Lyme was the cause of her issues. For Lyme disease to cause the kind of neurological issues that Kayleigh was experiencing she would need yet another test called a spinal tap. It was as bad as it sounds. They took a very large needle and inserted it into Kayleigh's back to take a sample of the fluid around her spine.

This was supposed to indicate whether the Lyme disease they'd found in her blood had crossed the blood-brain barrier and affected her neurologically.

The spinal tap came back negative for Lyme disease which they explained meant it could not be the source of her problems.

Back to square one.

The days all blended together until one morning when we got blindsided. Looking back, it certainly could have been much worse, but it did not seem like it at the time.

Every morning, the team of doctors doing their rounds would give us the status update for the day and what the game plan was as far as testing or treatment. This day started with one of the nurses telling us: "Kayleigh is being discharged. The doctor will be by with details."

The first thing I could think was *WTF? Discharged? She is NOT cured.* The first group of doctors came in. They were from neurology and said essentially, "We have no idea what is causing her symptoms but believe she is either faking it or Lyme is the cause." They further said, "There is nothing else we can do for her."

My frustration and anger grew. Faking it? You just said my daughter was faking it?

They clearly had no idea how miserable she was and seemed to not really care. I could not believe what I was hearing.

Later that day, the infectious disease doctors came in and explained that the negative spinal tap made it totally impossible for Lyme to have caused her issues. We were hearing one thing from some of the doctors and another thing from other doctors.

Katrina and I were upset, to put it mildly.

Our world had been turned upside down for our little girl and there was not a damn thing we could do about it. I have never felt more helpless in my life.

After many days and nights being there, we were no closer to finding out the cause of our daughter's condition. As a father, I have no greater instinct than to try and help my daughter by whatever means necessary—yet I could do little. These supposedly "best of the best" specialists had zero idea what was going on, and I had no idea how to help.

The next steps we had to take were like a swift kick in the nuts. We were definitely being discharged. The doctors were giving up. Katrina and I were both in complete shock. What could we do?

We had to do something.

It was time to fight.

Many options flashed through my head. Most of them were completely irrational and would likely have ended up with me in handcuffs. I felt absolutely helpless and utterly useless as a father. My little girl needed help. I had to do something.

I remembered seeing a number in a brochure for the patient advocacy office that worked for the executive team for the hospital. So, I found the number and called, hoping they could help.

After the call, the advocacy office sent down a group of managers to talk with us. I explained the scenario in detail, that we needed to stay, and that their expert doctors needed to figure this out NOW. The team left to talk to the doctors. Upon returning, they gave us the exact same story the doctors had. "There's nothing we can do" and, "They think she might be making it up." I was in complete and utter disbelief and again out of options.

Kayleigh was discharged and sent home with no expectations of getting better anytime soon. All we knew was that she had Lyme Disease, but it was not supposed to be causing her problems. The doctors gave her an antibiotic to take home to treat the Lyme. I could not believe they were sending her home. No next steps, no follow-ups, just a dismissive, "There is nothing we can do" and "Here's some antibiotics to take care of the Lyme disease but it won't fix her."

Then a week later what felt like a miracle happened: Despite all her medical professionals saying there was no possible way the Lyme disease could have caused her symptoms, they were wrong. Before Kayleigh had even finished the prescription, her symptoms were completely gone, and she was back to normal.

I was overjoyed she was better, yet still frustrated at all the pain, frustration, and confusion she'd had to go through.

WHAT DOES KAYLEIGH'S STORY HAVE TO DO WITH THE *RULES OF ENGAGEMENT*?

Let me explain.

The doctors started out on the right path and created a good plan. But they did not implement the plan well, and as time went on, they broke down and pointed fingers at each other. They were on completely different pages. This was because they did not establish their rules of engagement. They were each on their own path and were not united in solving the problem.

When defining the rules of engagement, it is important to focus on the mission first. The rules are written to help define a clear path to completing the mission regardless of what happens in the process.

These rules follow the same train of thought as your standard operating procedures (SOPs) for daily non-mission-specific tasks. This may sound complicated if you are not familiar with SOPs but the concept is very simple. Get clear on what you do, why you are doing it, and the specific methods you need to use.

When setting up your rules of engagement a few specifics should almost always be included, like the following:

TIMELINE (WHEN)

Set the expectation of how long it will take to complete the mission, including both best- and worst-case scenarios. Perhaps there is a drop-dead date or a time when certain tasks must be completed. In any case, be sure that the team is clear on what the timeline is for the entire mission, as well as any specific timelines that pertain to a particular portion of the mission that will be carried out by a particular group of the team or team member.

ASSIGNMENTS (WHO)

You must know who or what team is responsible for any given portion of the entire mission. Allowing people or teams to own their portion can be referred to as a decentralized command. Empowering teams or units to operate independently increases efficiency and ensures that each area of the mission keeps moving forward simultaneously.

TARGET (WHY)

This is arguably the most impactful segment of the ROE. While "When" and "Who" are important as they provide direction, but "Why" provides motivation and unites the team as a unit.

At this point, we have established the plan and the rules surrounding the implementation. The next step is communicating this information clearly and concisely to the team.

We will discuss that in the coming chapter, so make sure to keep reading!

We have covered a ton of content so far and it may seem overwhelming. But it doesn't have to be if you execute each of these steps one at a time.

I wrote this book to give you a complete blueprint for your business, but if you need help implementing what you are learning, my team and I are here to help. The best way to reach us is at

www.TacticalEntrepreneurAcademy.com/LetsTalk

TACTICAL TAKEAWAYS

- Without rules of engagement even a good plan can fail.

- Know your "When," "Who," and "Why."

- Desperate times require desperate measures.

CHAPTER SIX

RALLY THE TROOPS

"Few things can help an individual more than to place responsibility on him, and to let him know that you trust him."
—*Booker T. Washington*

In the last two chapters, we covered a lot of ground, from making the plan to establishing the rules of how the plan will be implemented.

That was a lot of work and must be the hardest part, right?

Wrong.

It's great that you have a plan and that you clearly understand your "When," "Who," and "Why." But guess what? No one else understands *a single part* of it.

Here's a prime example of why that matters.

MEET JOE

One of my clients, who we will call Joe, found himself in the following situation:

Joe had crushed finding his gap; he'd come up with an absolutely awesome plan and even had his rules of engagement laid out with surgical precision—which makes sense since Joe is a physician.

Joe set up a staff meeting and created an exquisite PowerPoint to lay out everything he'd dreamt up. It was pretty cool if you are into that kind of thing.

When it came time to communicate every pivotal detail to his team, that is where Joe went off track.

Because Joe is a crazy smart guy, he did not realize his patients and staff had a problem understanding him. He spoke way over everyone's head in most situations. This left everyone guessing as to what exactly Joe meant and what they were supposed to do.

He hadn't even gotten halfway through his presentation when one of his staff got the courage to explain that he had no idea what Joe was attempting to communicate. Many others chimed in with the same point, and it led to a great discussion, but Joe had to go back to the drawing board and devise a plan to get across what he needed.

On the plus side, Joe really dodged a bullet on the first version of his plan as the whole project could have failed miserably. Thankfully, because his staff stood up and told him about the issue, he got ahead of the problem. Many other leaders have not been so lucky.

RALLY ROUND

Now you know, it does matter if your plan and rules of engagement are perfect. Without clearly communicating every detail to your team, you have little chance of success. Let's now review some tips for rallying the troops to get them focused and provide them with the key information they need to perform their steps in the most effective way possible.

BELIEVING IS THE FIRST STEP

Get buy-in from the major players of your team. Hopefully, you took my previous advice and looped them in early to help with the plan. Keeping them on board is much easier when they are already deeply invested.

IDENTIFY YOUR AUDIENCE AND THEIR SUBJECT KNOWLEDGE

Do you remember when you were a kid and had to solve math problems using the "lowest common denominator?" This process is somewhat like that. We first need to know who our audience is and what their knowledge is on the subject at hand. This is not an assessment of their IQ. We're looking for how much they know about X topic and how often they have dealt with it in any given scenario.

Your critical information must be communicated in such a way that everyone understands.

BRIEF EVERYONE AT ONCE IF POSSIBLE

It is imperative that nothing gets lost in translation as you are relaying your plan. Remember the old telephone game where you would whisper a sentence to someone, they would whisper it to someone else and so on, until by the time it came back to you, the message was totally different? While that is an extreme example, the threat of miscommunication affecting the outcome is real.

INCLUDE ANY OF THE POSSIBLE OUTCOMES OF EACH PART OF THE MISSION

While you may not be able to cover every small detail, be sure to talk through the possible scenarios that might happen when you implement your plan. If your team has time to prepare for the unexpected, they will handle surprises much better with much less damage to your mission.

KEEP IT SIMPLE

Let me say that again because it's that important to remember. **Keep it simple**. The plan doesn't have to be any more complicated than it absolutely has to be. Simple means fast, easy-to-remember, and easy-to-implement.

SET CLEAR PRIORITIES

Each team member should not be deciding what they think is more important. In a perfect world, every aspect of your plan would be done exactly right, with every step complete 100%. But your team could, at any time, be put in a scenario where that just can't happen. So, be sure they know the best choice to make should they ever have to make it.

You've now reached the critical point in the mission. Success hangs in the balance, and the plan could go smoothly or hit rough patches. How you handle rallying the troops will make all the difference.

TACTICAL TAKEAWAYS

- Communication is key.
- Be sure everyone knows the plan.
- Get key stakeholders on board early.
- Keep it simple.

Remember we are here if you need any help making these changes to your business. Be sure to check out our website at www.TacticalEntrepreneurAcademy.com for more tips, tricks, and techniques. Need more help than that? We have group and individual coaching programs available that focus on expert training. You are not alone. We Got Your Six.

CHAPTER SEVEN

EXECUTE

"Strategy is important, but execution is everything. Incredibly successful people focus on executing incredibly well."
—*Jeff Haden*

Now that the plan has been formulated, the rules of engagement have been communicated, and the troops are on board, it is time to execute the plan.

We are once again at a fork in the road.

While you have come far from where you started, there is still much more to do correctly. Even with the best-laid plan, the mission can get compromised and end badly. There is no clear assurance of victory.

That said, you will want to avoid some pitfalls.

We will take a look at those in detail shortly, but first, I want to share a story with you.

This story is about how results can be based on execution. It also covers what can happen if you don't execute. Be sure to read this story closely as there are many hidden gems of knowledge embedded in it.

An Effective Execution

In good times, when business is moving at a normal speed, it is important to make decisions in a timely and effective manner. When markets are volatile, it's even more critical.

One example of volatility that we can all relate to happened when Covid-19 first appeared. Although we may not see this scenario again in our lifetimes, it affected so many businesses and completely turned our lives upside down. Covid-19 created many hardships for businesses, but it also created many opportunities.

In March of 2020, the firearms industry saw the biggest surge in guns and ammunition sales in history. More new gun owners than ever before emerged, too. By the beginning of April, shelves were empty. Distributors in the industry and many manufacturers scrambled to replenish their stock. Over the next weeks, our buyers at

Sheepdog got our shelves somewhat restocked. Then the George Floyd looting and riots began.

A few weeks later, Sheepdog saw a surge in sales that met or exceeded sales during the Covid-19 lockdown. We had never seen anything like it before. This was a frenzy of scared people trying to get what they needed to protect their families. People realized they couldn't rely on the police to always be there, that as individuals, they had to take responsibility for the safety of their families. We also saw a huge rush on sales of our first-aid and medic kits and our emergency first aid classes.

With the second surge cleaning us almost out of all product, we had two options. We could close for a while until society returned to normal, or we could find a gap and run through it as ferociously as possible.

Ownership met and decided that instead of lying down like many of the gun shops in our area, we would lead the way and get our hands on everything we could to keep our Sheepdog family of customers supplied. We came up with a plan, set the rules of engagement, and rallied the troops. Then, it was time to execute.

Over the next months, our buyers deployed the plan with sniper-like precision. Every morning they were on the phone with all our vendors asking what had come in overnight and what could be set aside for us. During that time, many other area shops waited for vendors to call them. Many shut down or substantially reduced hours and were not too concerned about scraping up product.

Our buyers had everything they required and any authorization to do whatever it took to get us product. Vendors had pallets of product for us, but shipping was backed up.

No problem.

Our buyers found a truck and sent two of our armed guards from our security company on a road trip. If our buyers had a hard time reaching a certain company rep, they would send Chicago style pizza (which is, of course, the greatest pizza in the United States and possibly the world) and a note. The next thing you knew, they were back in touch with their contacts just by offering a simple gesture of thanks.

While I love to brag on our team over at Sheepdog Firearms, that is not why I chose this example. I chose it because it was some of the best execution I have ever seen by any team for any mission. What our team did made a huge difference in our business and, more importantly, in our ability to properly equip our customers. These actions over time created the foundation of who we are today.

WHAT IF IT HADN'T WORKED?

We also need to remember that this plan easily could have gone in a different direction. We might have needed to shut our doors for a while. We might have had to lay off some employees. Had our buyers not executed so well, or even if they had simply hesitated to make some of these pivotal decisions, the end result could have been very different. I'm sure you learned some lessons from that story. Let's recap them now.

MOVE SWIFTLY AND WITH PURPOSE

Do not hesitate. When the plan is put into motion, there is no time for second-guessing leadership or trying to figure out a better way. The results will be evaluated at a predetermined time. Even if every little segment of your plan does not go perfectly, you will be 100% further along than if you waited.

FOLLOW THE PLAN. FOLLOW THE PLAN. FOLLOW THE PLAN

I often see clients make the mistake of over-thinking. There is a time for thinking, and there is a time for doing. This is the time for doing.

Don't Make Excuses

You will be successful, or you will learn. Those are the only two possible options for any given scenario. Excuses are simply lies that we make up when we are not ready to learn the lesson(s) from our failures.

With your plan executed, you should have completed your mission or at least moved closer to completing it. Sometimes, missions are ongoing and will be a constant work in progress.

When your mission is complete, it is then time to take a breath, step back, and fully assess the outcome and how your team executed the mission.

Taking a deep dive into both of these aspects is game-changing for the next time you make a plan. There is pure gold in the lessons you will learn. These can include the answers to questions like: *Do I have the right team in place? Could we have done anything different? How can we further improve our processes? How can we become even more efficient?*

Too often, when we achieve a target, we do not take the time to assess our process. We might assume that everything must have been done right as the mission was completed successfully. But that is rarely the case. While done is better than perfect, it does not mean that actions cannot be sharpened to get them a bit closer to perfect.

Results rarely stay the same.
You are either getting better or getting worse.
Let's choose to move forward daily one step at a time.

Next, we'll take a close look into refining your efforts. But before we do, remember what you've learned in this chapter:

TACTICAL TAKEAWAYS

- Execution matters.

- Move swiftly with purpose.

- Follow the plan.

- Don't make excuses.

CHAPTER EIGHT

ASSESS AND MODIFY

"The pessimist complains about the wind;
the optimist expects it to change;
the realist adjusts the sails."
—William Arthur Ward

There are multiple ways to view the outcome of any given situation.

The first and most valuable lens we can look through is "Did we complete our mission?" or "Did we achieve our target?" After answering those questions, the next step is to move down a level. "What did we execute well?" "What did we execute poorly?" Finally, we need to ask, "What can be improved upon?"

Asking and answering those questions honestly provides a wealth of information that can be used to improve in all areas.

I'll cover more on this topic, but first, I want to share a story of success lived by a man named Bob. Read on to learn how his success was compounded and amplified.

AMPLIFYING SUCCESS

It was March of 2020, and President Trump had just spoken on Covid-19. Everything began to shut down as lockdowns were issued across the nation.

Bob had been in business for just over eight years. He had three locations, and his business was in rapid growth mode. His restaurants served premium pub food. They included all the normal staples of burgers, fries, wings, flatbreads, cheese curds, and other goodness. His menu options were varied, and his food was amazingly delicious. Bob always used the best ingredients, and that transferred into the taste of his food. Bob had a plan in place to grow, and his team was doing a great job on implementation. It was quite exciting to watch.

At that time, Bob had very little takeout business, and he was not aligned with any delivery service. He focused on bringing people into the restaurants as they made fun places to hang out and were known for their tasty selection of craft beer. His restaurants were always packed most evenings and every weekend.

Bob's business was going very well before Covid-19 came to town.

Then in a rush, businesses were shut down, with only those deemed "essential" allowed to remain open. Because of where Bob was located, he could stay operational, but he could only provide carryout. Remember, at this time, Bob was doing very little carryout. This put him in a situation where he urgently needed to figure out what to do next. When he assessed the facts, it became clear that the world's circumstances weren't going away anytime soon.

He knew his current plan was not going to work. Because of his success, Bob was lucky enough to have fairly deep pockets that could enable him to keep going one way or another.

He could have just shut down since he estimated that his cash reserves would have lasted him 10-12 months. But the thought of burning through the money he had worked so hard for did not sit well with Bob. Closing up shop was not an option in his mind.

Bob got to work assessing the way his locations had been operating. He thought through what needed to change so he could successfully pivot into the takeout market. He researched the food delivery services he could partner with and crunched the numbers. The takeout portion made sense number-wise, but the food delivery partners didn't.

The percentage of the order they were getting back was too high. Bob was in a pickle and not sure what to do. He needed the additional sales from delivery services to keep up his volume enough so he could continue to buy the same amounts of ingredients to allow him to keep his current pricing.

Then it hit him!

He had a ton of extra staff who would not be needed when inside dining was shut down. Rather than lay off those workers, he decided to use them to staff his own delivery service.

Bob knew he had to move fast to capitalize on this opportunity. He formulated a plan and drew everything out to visually show his staff. He involved his head chef, front-of-the-house managers, and the other key employees in the process. Doing so made them buy-in that much more. They all loved that Bob was taking charge and doing everything he could for the restaurants and his staff. Many of the employees had been with him from the beginning, so they were deeply invested in the restaurant's success thus far.

Bob also knew that each of the locations was a bit different and would need modifications to the plan. Bob and his team made the changes and presented the plan to the staff. Each location had a team meeting where Bob, along with the other stakeholders, communicated the plan. It was very well received, but there was a ton of work to be done.

Within two weeks, everyone on the team was ready for a soft launch of the new delivery service. The website was modified to show the new delivery option. The marketing team blitzed all their social media and email lists, and Facebook ads ran. You could see the buy-in evident in the employees' excitement. Even the wait staff who had been converted to delivery drivers were excited to go out and see their patrons.

The soft launch went fairly smoothly. There were a few adjustments made, but nothing major as the plan was solid and the team executed.

Within four weeks of the launch, the delivery business had grown to surpass the takeout business. Along with all the other changes, Bob's head chef decided to create family meals. These were pre-chosen packages that fed a family of four and provided a great value. With the attractive price and easy way to order, the family meals were an absolute hit. The customers also loved that there was no customization necessary as all toppings came on the side—so everyone was happy. This option was so popular that many of the local competitors attempted their own knockoffs.

Bob's example illustrates that sometimes even when a plan is going well, it requires big changes when an out-of-control event happens. The sooner you realize the problem to solve, assess the situation and implement a plan to fix it, the better off you will be. Changes can be required long after a plan is put into motion, like Bob found out, or you might need to apply them immediately when launching. The point is to always keep your eyes open and your head on a swivel. There is room for improvement in any plan, regardless of the situation.

LET THE MACHINE RUN

After making any needed changes, it's time to let the machine run and see what happens. If you want to be successful long term, you must continue to evolve. There is no such thing as standing still or staying the same. Business is always moving forward or sliding back. When you listen to your customers and the market, you can set yourself up to win in any environment.

Hopefully, this example impacted you to remember the importance of the ongoing improvement process —and that you are truly never done.

There will be times of huge change and times of little change, but the most important parts of the process will continue to operate. Always pay attention to what is changing in your market and be ready to act at a moment's notice.

People often think that the biggest gains made in business happen when you take the time to work out a plan in painstaking detail, slowly but surely getting every last consideration completely perfect. The opposite is actually true.

The biggest successes are often centered around taking imperfect action. Rapid execution beats a perfect plan every time.

When my competition is planning, I am acting and getting out in the marketplace, enabling early sales capture. But what is even more important is that through planning, I get to test my strategies before the competition even goes to market. Sometimes my initial ideas are spot on, and other times I do a 180 shortly after a launch. Having the extra time to adjust makes an impactful difference in the long run.

TACTICAL TAKEAWAYS

- There is always room to get better.

- Details matter.

- Ongoing Improvement is the key to long-term success.

- Know your market.

Ready to adapt and overcome to take your business to the next level?

Check out TacticalEntrepreneurAcademy.com for everything from online courses to one-on-one coaching.

We Got Your Six.

CHAPTER NINE

FINAL THOUGHTS

"Don't expect front row seats if
you're giving nosebleed effort."
—Eric Thomas

Like most things in life, what you put into your process will determine what you get out of it.

As I revealed all the way back in Chapter One, there is no secret sauce to do the work for you. What I can assure you is that success is simple but not easy.

But if you follow the processes outlined in this book, and do the work, the results will come.

So many people are stuck on the method they have always followed and are unwilling to change or evolve. Sadly, their businesses will likely be destroyed by natural disasters, or they will fade away on their own. Many will have been around for 10, 20, and even 30 years, but during that time, they will have never changed a step in their process. I certainly have great respect for tradition, but when it comes to business, it's often *evolve or die.*

As an entrepreneur, father, grandfather, and husband, I often ask myself serious questions. In being totally honest, the questions will lead to a conversation of sorts with myself.

These questions start out harmless enough but often end up taking me down a rabbit hole, where I ask myself why I am doing what I am doing. Then they go deeper to *why am I here?* and *what is my Purpose?* The grand finale of those questions is *what am I leaving behind as my LEGACY?*

These are all very personal and meaningful questions that must be answered. Our answers may not be exactly the same, but I would bet most entrepreneurs would answer these questions pretty similarly.

Your business is your chance to leave an impact on the world long after you are dust. What you are building can literally evade death and transcend time.

It can allow you to live well beyond your years.

It can provide a gift beyond all others—insight you can give to your great, great, great-grandchildren.

You might be thinking *not my little business*, but you could not be more wrong. Most huge businesses today started out small with a dream as their owners toiled away in a basement or garage. Do names like Amazon, Microsoft, Apple, or Google sound familiar? That's how they all got their start.

Ready to get tactical on growing your business and creating your legacy? You don't have to go it alone. Let's talk about how we can help.

Head to:
TacticalEntrepreneurAcademy.com/LetsTalk

Dream big and do the work.

Your business could be the next titan to rise.

ACKNOWLEDGMENTS

First, I would like to thank my Apex family. Without the inspiration of each of you provided there is no way this book would have ever made it to paper. I would like to offer an extra thanks to Ryan Stewman, Thomas Keenan, and Drewbie Wilson for helping me become a version of myself I would not have imagined possible.

I would also like to thank my business partner Jimm Shepard. There is no one I would rather have beside me in the boardroom or any other battleground.

I would like to say thank you to all of the Sheepdog family. This includes our dedicated staff, and loyal customers. Without all of you the vision of Sheepdog Firearms is nothing but a dream. Through your hard work and dedication, we are changing an industry.

I want to thank my simply amazing editor Hilary Jastram at J Hil Creative. She went above and beyond my expectations making the process easier than I had imagined. Her calming and confident demeanor was just what this author needed to complete one of the most demanding projects I have ever taken on.

I would like to thank my parents Rich and Helen for their support over the years. I am grateful to have you both in my corner. I appreciate you always being there to cheer me on even when you thought my ideas were crazy.

Last but certainly not least, I would like to thank my beautiful wife Katrina for being there through it all. I look back over our 25 years of marriage, and raising our three awesome children, and I am simply astounded by our journey together. I am grateful for the tough times, for the challenges and for the hard roads we traveled and that you were by my side the whole way. I would not be the man I am today without you, Katrina.

About the Author

Steve Schabacker is best known for his startups in the Information technology space, but his experience goes much deeper. He is the definition of a serial entrepreneur, having been a part of over a dozen startups in many different industries. Steve is an expert in many areas of security, including physical, electronic, and cyber security planning. His current holdings include firearms retail stores, a training center, a security and investigations firm, and a custom firearm manufacturer, as well as other investments.

While Steve enjoys business, his driving force is his family. He and his wife Katrina have been married for 25 years and have three adult children (Kayleigh, Christian, and Kendra), a grandson (Brantley), and two four-legged children named Finn and Daisy.

He and his family reside in Chicagoland, where they enjoy live music, traveling, and making memories.

DISCLAIMER

Although the publisher and the author have made every effort to ensure that the information in this book was correct at press time and while this publication is designed to provide accurate information in regard to the subject matter covered, the publisher and the author assume no responsibility for errors, inaccuracies, omissions, or any other inconsistencies herein and hereby disclaim any liability to any party for any loss, damage, or disruption caused by errors or omissions, whether such errors or omissions result from negligence, accident, or any other cause.

Unless otherwise indicated, all the names, characters, businesses, places, events and incidents in this book are either the product of the author's imagination or used in a fictitious manner. Any resemblance to actual persons, living or dead, or actual events is purely coincidental.

The publisher and the author do not make any guarantee or other promise as to any results that may be obtained from using the content of this book. To the maximum extent permitted by law, the publisher and the author disclaim any and all liability in the event any information, commentary, analysis, opinions, advice and/

or recommendations contained in this book prove to be inaccurate, incomplete or unreliable, or result in any investment or other losses.

Made in the USA
Monee, IL
29 April 2022